INTRODUCTION

I was having lunch recently with a friend whose business takes him to the far corners of the globe, and he told me he was having a wonderful time with his snow. All were rescued alive! In Helsinki I was ushered into the office of our branch man and there were two Shepherds lying beside his desk. They come to

The German Shepherd Dog, known as the the Deutsche Schaferhund in Germany and the Alsatian in Great Britain, is a recognizable face throughout the world.

first German Shepherd Dog.

"I thought you were just giving me the old build-up," he said, "but it's true. Shepherds are all over the world. I'm just back from a six-week world trip, and I've seen them everywhere. In Switzerland I saw a platoon of Shepherds locating and helping to dig out members of a ski party buried in a snow avalanche. The dogs found every man, even those who were buried under 20 feet of

work with him every day. Then in Lima, our man couldn't meet me at the airport. He was delayed at a far... on a cla... him snapshots of my family, our Shepherd sitting right in the front row, of course. He suggested that I must steal a peek at his twin sons—already gone to bed. So I did. They were all right, sound asleep in an enormous bed, and right smack between the two kids was a beautiful German Shepherd. My Hindu host explained the oversized bed. Seems that the dog and the children were inseparable, so it had been necessary to get the big bed made in order to accommodate all three!"

And so it goes. For truly the German Shepherd is an international favorite, and he fills many different jobs, too. Sometimes you see him working at his original job of herding cattle or sheep. Sometimes he is a movie star. And because of his fabulous capacity for highly specialized training, he is used extensively by state and municipal police in criminal work, tracking and rescue, as well as for the detection of hidden contraband.

His nose and his brain are so keen that he can locate buried metal, concealed narcotics, or illegal distilling operations. He has notable use with the Royal Canadian Mounted Police. Such is his capacity for special training that he is naturally acceptable in the US Armed Services where he is used as sentry dog, communications runner, or as a casualty spotter where he learns to seek out and "report" the presence and location of personnel who are injured and unconscious and might otherwise be left for dead. And in one of his most spectacular and most

Herding sheep and goats was the original purpose of the German Shepherd Dog: in this field he excelled as a competent shepherd's assistant and nighttime watchman. Today the breed's instincts are still very much intact.

ISABELLE FRANÇAIS

As a watchdog, guard dog and protector, the German Shepherd enjoys a reputation that is second to none.

moving roles, we find the Shepherd being the eyes and devoted companion of a blind master.

For all the varied roles he fills in what we might call "public service to mankind," the German Shepherd's greatest love and starring role is that of being a devoted "family" dog. Here all the wonderful qualities that have made him famous come quietly into full scope. Here he is the children's playmate, full of fun and face-licking but always with a keen protective "radar" at work so no harm befalls *his* children. Here, as a house dog, he fully uses his almost fanatical love and affection and protective instinct for you, your family and friends. He'll roughhouse with you or lie in quiet, dignified adoration. And his keen senses miss nothing. At night he'll hear and investigate strange sounds you can't even hear. Thieves and other evil-doers cannot operate where there's a Shepherd on the job!

Those of us who like dogs usually have a soft spot for *all* dogs. However, I can tell you, in all sincerity, if you have never owned a German Shepherd Dog, you have missed one of life's greatest pleasures. You haven't really lived until you and your family have been owned by one!

Due to the breed's versatility and intelligence, the German Shepherd ranks among the most trainable of all dogs.

ORIGIN AND HISTORY

For years, the German Shepherd was referred to as a "Police Dog." There is *no* such breed as "Police Dog." Any dog of any breed is a police dog if it is trained to perform police work. It is not a matter of breed but of training. The American Kennel Club officially terms our breed German Shepherd Dog, a literal translation of "Deutsche almost without exception, were bred and kept for economic reasons, as well as for protection. Hounds, for example, were first used to procure meat. And there were also the herding dogs who helped in the management and protection of flocks and herds, as well as the owner's person, home, family, and property.

In Germany there was an old,

A trotting breed, the German Shepherd is a swift-moving, athletic dog with much to recommend him as a sturdy outdoor dog.

ISABELLE FRANCAIS

Schäferhund," which it is called in the country of its origin. While it is called the "Alsatian" in England, other languages keep to a translation of the original name.

DOG'S PLACE IN MAN'S LIFE

Due to selective breeding and geographical separation, no race of domestic animals occurs in so many breeds, shapes, sizes, and colors as do our dogs. While many have been produced solely for pets and exhibiting, the oldest breeds, old race of shepherd dogs widely used throughout that and neighboring lands. No one really knew just how old the breed was. It had seemingly always been there. While it varied a good deal as to size, coat, and coloring, still wherever it was found it was readily recognized as a special type.

About the middle of the 19th century, this amazing race of shepherd dogs came under the study of one Max von Stephanitz, a cavalry officer and brilliant student of animal genetics. Here, he observed, was a race of dogs having great natural beauty coupled with fantastically acute intelligence and senses. These dogs seemed to think, to use judgment entirely apart from anything they had been taught to do. Without directions of any kind, this shepherd dog would seek out a freezing newborn lamb and tenderly pick it up and carry it to his owner. This same dog could destroy or drive off animals much larger than itself if they threatened the flock. The dog knew what to do when sheep strayed into cultivated fields. Without command and entirely of his own volition, this dog would either circle the flock or go straight across their backs to force the wandering ones back into the flock. He knew when to string out the flock to cross a narrow bridge, and he knew when to bunch up the sheep again after crossing. And all this with the barest minimum of training and the most haphazard breeding.

BREEDING STANDARDS SET

Captain von Stephanitz resolved on a plan and assembled a group of friends to discuss it with them. Just think, he told them, what could be done. Set a goal in the form of a standard of excellence and breed these dogs

Breed type has been essentially set for generations of German Shepherds. Today, although there are variations in coat and size, the GSD continues to breed true.

according to the strictest rules, keeping careful records of what individuals regularly produced which characteristics in their offspring. Breed ever so carefully, only from the best, and keep it up *permanently.* Constantly standardize and improve the physical type of the dog; but, even more important, further develop and always keep that uncanny brain, that "natural" judgment, those acute senses, always toward the standard of excellence. Set up an organization to foster, direct, and record this great project. Do this, he told his friends, and here will be a breed of dogs unequalled!

And so this group drew up the standard of excellence and incorporated it into the Verein fur Deutsche Schaferhund. Through the work done and continued by this organization, the German Shepherd Dog Club of America, and by breed clubs in other parts of the world, we have the superb, standard-bred German Shepherd Dog as we know him today.

ISABELLE FRANCAIS

Breeders thrive to maintain, and ultimately improve, type and temperament with every litter.

At six weeks of age, this German Shepherd puppy is curious and active.

ISABELLE FRANCAIS

No German Shepherd Dog is perfect when compared to the breed standard, though each dog has certain features which viewed individually are flawless. These two lovely Shepherds are Ghalain and Micheala.

ISABELLE FRANCAIS

DESCRIPTION OF THE BREED

The standard of a breed is the criterion by which the appearance (and to a certain extent, the temperament) of any given dog is made subject, as far as possible, to objective measurement. Basically the standard for any breed is a definition of the perfect dog, to which all specimens of the breed are compared; the degree of excellence of the appearance of a given dog for conformation show purposes is in direct proportion to the dog's agreement with the requirements of the standard for its breed. Necessarily, of course, a certain amount of subjective evaluation is involved because of the wording of the standard itself and because of the factors introduced through the completely human judging apparatus. Breed standards are always subject to change through review by the national breed club for each dog, so it is always wise

The stance of the German Shepherd Dog makes the breed unique from all other breeds. Notice the extended hind leg showing the correct angle of the hock (ankle) and the flow of the topline (along the back).

ISABELLE FRANCAIS

Ch. Altana's Mystique, owned by Jane Firestone and handled by Jimmy Moses, retired after her Best of Breed win at Westminster in 1995 as the number one show dog of all time, having won 274 Best in Show victories.

ISABELLE FRANCAIS

BACK
Straight, strongly developed, relatively short.

HINDQUARTERS
Broad, well-muscled thighs.

METATARSUS
Short, strong and tightly articulated.

TAIL
Bushy, set low, curved like a saber.

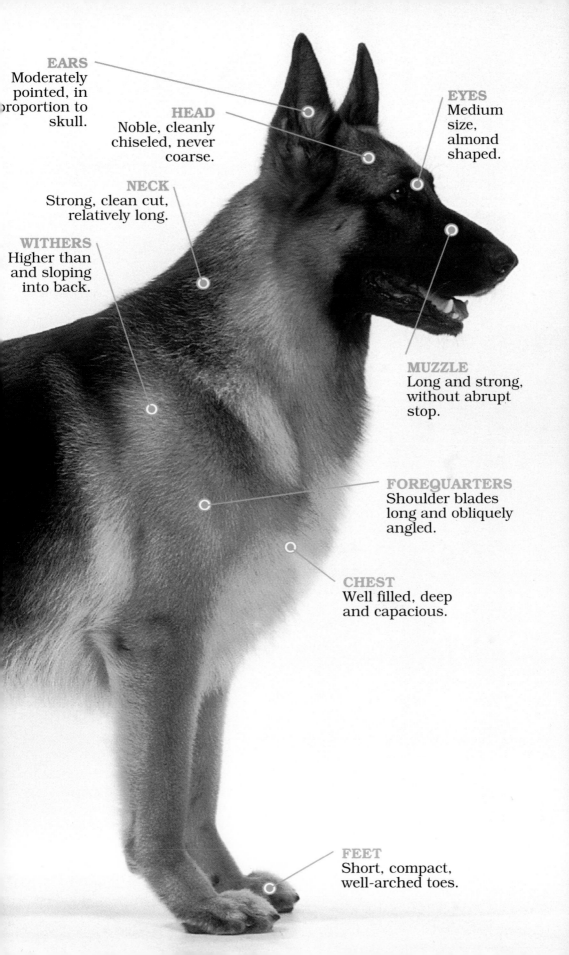

EARS
Moderately pointed, in proportion to skull.

HEAD
Noble, cleanly chiseled, never coarse.

EYES
Medium size, almond shaped.

NECK
Strong, clean cut, relatively long.

WITHERS
Higher than and sloping into back.

MUZZLE
Long and strong, without abrupt stop.

FOREQUARTERS
Shoulder blades long and obliquely angled.

CHEST
Well filled, deep and capacious.

FEET
Short, compact, well-arched toes.

Dogs 24 to 26 inches; bitches 22 to 24 inches.

HEIGHT (from shoulder to floor)

ISABELLE FRANCAIS

Ch. Altana's Mystique, owned by Jane A. Firestone.

kennel club. The following is a version of the official standard for the German Shepherd Dog.

THE BREED STANDARD

General Appearance— The first impression of a good German Shepherd Dog is that of a strong, agile, well-muscled animal, alert and full of life. It is well balanced, with harmonious development of the forequarter and hindquarter. The dog is longer than tall, deep bodied, and presents an outline of smooth curves rather than angles. It looks substantial and not spindly, giving the impression, both at rest and in motion, of muscular firmness and nimbleness without any look of clumsiness or soft living. The ideal dog is stamped with a look of quality and nobility—difficult to define, but unmistakable when present. Secondary sex characteristics are strongly marked, and every animal gives a definite impression of masculinity or feminity, according to its sex.

Size, Proportion, Substance— The desired *height* for males at the top of the highest point of the shoulder blade is 24 to 26 inches; and for bitches, 22 to 24 inches. The German Shepherd Dog is longer than tall, with the most desirable *proportion* as 10 to 8 $^1/_2$. The length is measured from the point of the prosternum or breastbone to the rear edge of the pelvis, the ischial tuberosity. The desirable long proportion is not derived from a long back, but from overall length with relation to height, which is achieved by length of forequarter and length of

to keep up with developments in a breed by checking the publications of your national

German Shepherd's ears should be carried parallel to each other and not tilted inwards. Illustration by John Quinn.

withers and hindquarter, viewed from the side.

Head—The **head** is noble, cleanly chiseled, strong without coarseness, but above all not fine, and in proportion to the body. The head of the male is distinctly masculine, and that of the bitch distinctly feminine. The **expression** is keen, intelligent and composed. **Eyes** of medium size, almond shaped, set a little obliquely and not protruding. The color is as dark as possible. **Ears** are moderately pointed, in proportion to the skull, open toward the front, and carried erect when at attention, the ideal carriage being one in which the center lines of the ears, viewed from the front, are parallel to each other and perpendicular to the ground. A dog with cropped or hanging ears must be *disqualified*. Seen from the front the forehead is only moderately arched, and the **skull** slopes into the long, wedge-shaped muzzle without abrupt stop. The **muzzle** is long and strong, and its topline is parallel to the topline of the skull. **Nose** black. A dog with a nose that is not predominantly black must be *disqualified*. The lips are firmly fitted. Jaws are strongly developed. **Teeth**— 42 in number—20 upper and 22 lower—are strongly developed and meet in a scissors bite in which part of the inner surface of the upper incissors meet and engage part of the outer surface of the lower incisors. An overshot jaw or a level bite is undesirable. An undershot jaw is a *disqualifying fault*. Complete dentition is to be preferred. Any missing teeth other than first premolars is a *serious fault*.

Neck, Topline, Body— The **neck** is strong and muscular, clean-cut and relatively long, proportionate in size to the head and without loose folds of skin.

An undershot jaw is a disqualification. Illustration by John Quinn.

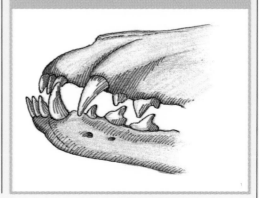

The German Shepherd's head is noble and cleanly chiseled; the expression is keen, intelligent and composed. The bitch's head is distinctly feminine as this lovely lady, Ch. Altana's Mystique, gracefully conveys.

When the dog is at attention or excited, the head is raised and the neck carried high; otherwise typical carriage of the head is forward rather than up and but little higher than the top of the shoulders, particularly in motion. **Topline**— The **withers** are higher than and sloping into the level back. The **back** is straight, very strongly developed without sag or roach, and relatively short. The whole structure of the **body** gives an impression of depth and solidity without bulkiness. **Chest**— Commencing at the prosternum, it is well filled and carried well down between the legs. It is deep and capacious, never shallow, with ample room for lungs and heart, carried well forward, with the prosternum showing ahead of the shoulder in profile. **Ribs** well sprung and long, neither barrel-shaped nor too flat, and carried down to a sternum which reaches to the elbows. Correct ribbing allows the elbows to move back freely when the dog is at a trot. Too round causes interference and throws the elbows out; too flat or short causes pinched elbows. Ribbing is carried well back so that the loin is relatively short. **Abdomen** firmly held and not paunchy. The bottom line is only moderately tucked up in the loin. **Loin—** Viewed from the top, broad and strong. Undue length between the last rib and the thigh, when viewed from the side, is undesirable. **Croup** long and gradually sloping. **Tail** bushy, with the last vertebra extended at least to the hock joint. It is set smoothly into the croup and low rather than high. At rest, the tail hangs in a slight curve like a saber. A slight hook— sometimes carried to one side— is faulty only to the extent that it mars general appearance. When the dog is excited or in motion, the curve is accentuated and the tail raised, but it should never be curled forward beyond a vertical line. Tails too short, or with clumpy ends due to ankylosis, are *serious faults*. A dog with a docked tail must be *disqualified*.

The back should be straight, never roach. Illustration by John Quinn.

Forequarters— The shoulder blades are long and obliquely angled, laid on flat and not placed forward. The upper arm joins the shoulder blade at about a right angle. Both the upper arm and the shoulder blade are well muscled. The forelegs, viewed from all sides, are straight and the bone oval rather than round. The pasterns are strong and springy and angulated at approximately a 25-degree angle from the vertical. Dewclaws on the forelegs may be removed, but are normally left on. The **feet** are short, compact with toes well arched, pads thick and firm, nails short and dark.

Hindquarters— The whole assembly of the thigh, viewed from the side, is broad with both upper and lower thigh well muscled, forming as nearly as possible a right angle. The upper thigh bone parallels the shoulder blade while the lower thigh bone parallels the upper arm. The metatarsus (the unit between the hock joint and the foot) is short, strong and tightly articulated. The dewclaws, if any, should be removed from the hind legs. Feet as in front.

Coat— The ideal dog has a double coat of medium length. The outer coat should be as dense as possible, hair straight, harsh and lying close to the body. A slightly wavy outer coat, often of wiry texture, is permissible. The head, including the inner ear and foreface, and the legs and paws are covered with short hair, and the neck with longer and thicker hair. The rear of the forelegs and hind legs has somewhat longer hair extending to the pasterns and hock, respectively. *Faults* in the coat include soft, silky, too long outer coat, woolly, curly and open coat.

Color— The German Shepherd Dog varies in color, and most colors are permissible. Strong rich colors are preferred. Pale,

The preferred colors in the German Shepherd are strong and rich, never washed out or pale. This puppy shows great promise with his deep pigment.

Although white German Shepherds have many adoring fans, none of them can be found in the AKC show ring, as white is a disqualification according to the breed standard.

washed-out colors and blues or livers are *serious faults*. A white dog must be *disqualified*.

Gait— A German Shepherd Dog is a trotting dog, and its structure has been developed to meet the requirements of its work. *General Impression*— The gait is outreaching, elastic, seemingly without effort, smooth and rhythmic, covering the maximum amount of ground with the minimum number of steps. At a walk it covers a great deal of ground, with long strides of both hind legs and forelegs. At a trot the dog covers still more ground with even longer stride, and moves powerfully but easily, with coordination and balance so that the gait appears to be the steady

ISABELLE FRANCAIS

The German Shepherd's coat is medium in length and as dense as possible, harsh but lying close to the body.

motion of a well-lubricated machine. The feet travel close to the ground on both forward reach and backward push. In order to achieve movement of this kind, there must be good muscular development and ligamentation. The hindquarters deliver, through the back, a powerful forward thrust which slightly lifts the whole animal and drives the body forward. Reaching far under, and passing the imprint left by the front foot, the hind foot takes hold of the ground; then hock, stifle and upper thigh come into play and sweep back, the stroke of the hind leg finishing with the foot still close to the ground in a smooth follow-through. The over-

The German Shepherd must be suited for the work that the breed was originally intended for. An efficient gait was tantamount to survival for a working sheepdog who needed to cover a large amount of ground in as few steps as possible.

ISABELLE FRANCAIS

reach of the hindquarter usually necessitates one hind foot passing outside and the other hind foot passing inside the track of the forefeet, and such action is not faulty unless the locomotion is crabwise with the dog's body sideways out of the normal straight line. ***Transmission***—The typical smooth, flowing gait is maintained with great strength and firmness of the back. The should reach out close to the ground in a long stride in harmony with that of the hindquarters. The dog does not track on widely separated parallel lines, but brings the feet inward toward the middle line of the body when trotting, in order to maintain balance. The feet track closely but do not strike or cross over. Viewed from the front, the front legs function from the

ROBERT SMITH

At a full trot, the back must remain firm and level. The feet are brought inward toward the middle line of the body without crossing over or striking.

whole effort of the hindquarter is transmitted to the forequarter through the loin, back and withers. At full trot, the back must remain firm and level without sway, roll, whip or roach. Unlevel topline with withers lower than the hip is a *fault*. To compensate for the forward motion imparted by the hindquarters, the shoulder should open to its full extent. The forelegs shoulder joint to the pad in a straight line. Viewed from the rear, the hind legs function from the hip joint to the pad in a straight line. Faults of gait, whether from front, rear, or side, are to be considered *very serious faults*.

Temperament— The breed has a distinct personality marked by direct and fearless, but not hostile, expression, self-confidence and a certain aloofness that does not lend itself to immediate and indiscriminate friendships. The dog must be approachable, quietly standing its ground and showing confidence and willingness to meet overtures without itself making them. It is poised, but when the occasion demands, eager and alert; both fit and willing to serve in its capacity as companion, watchdog, blind leader, herding dog, or guardian, whichever the circumstances may demand. The dog must not be timid, shrinking behind its master or handler; it should not be nervous, looking about or upward with anxious expression or showing nervous reactions, such as tucking of tail, to strange sounds or sights. Lack of confidence under any surroundings is not typical of good character. Any of the above deficiencies in character which indicate shyness must be penalized as *very serious faults* and any dog exhibiting pronounced indications of these must be excused from the ring. It must be possible for the judge to observe the teeth and to determine that both testicles are descended. Any dog that attempts to bite the judge must be *disqualified.* The ideal dog is a working animal with an incorruptible character combined with body and gait suitable for the arduous work that constitutes its primary purpose.

Disqualifications

Cropped or hanging ears.

Dogs with noses not predominantly black.

Undershot jaw.

Docked tail.

White dogs.

Any dog that attempts to bite the judge.

Mystique shows off her smooth, flowing gait.

A devoted companion for one and all, the German Shepherd has graced its way into many loving families.

TEMPERAMENT AND PERSONALITY

Rich man, poor man, and way stations in between, just ask any owner of a German Shepherd why he has one. Sure, he was probably first attracted to the breed by its great physical beauty. But no matter what language he speaks, or what his choice of words to describe it, you'll hear that the *character* of the German Shepherd is even more wonderful than its appearance.

Character, as the dictionary will tell you, is individuality, personality, qualities, and differences that add up to make a thing unique and distinctive. That is the German Shepherd in your home. Possessor of a brilliant heritage, he is a current edition of the sum total that has made his breed famous the world over.

Although less frequently seen, solid black German Shepherds possess all the same charms and talents of their sable and black and tan brethren.

KAREN TAYLOR

DEVOTION TO HIS FAMILY

Probably the German Shepherd's most outstanding characteristic is his devotion and adoration of his human family. It is an undeserving devotion that pervades every moment of the dog's life with you. It is a devotion to you and yours that is almost beyond human understanding in its extent and depth. And this devotion, plus uncanny intelligence, is quite logically coupled with the boundless urge to take care of you, to protect you— no matter what.

Does that sound like too much flowery talk? Well, then consider one instance (and I can give you thousands) of a German Shepherd guiding his sightless master around city streets all day without once indicating or flinching from the acute pain caused by a piece of sharp wire through his paw. Never did the pain deter the dog for one instant from the careful protection of his master from traffic, curbs, steps, and crowds.

Take another instance. Recently, out of hundreds of nominations (and a large percentage were German Shepherds), the National Dog Hero award was given to a German Shepherd. Why? The dog, then under a year old, had been purchased only a few weeks before the event. He was in the backyard with his owners when all of a sudden he rushed for the back door, tearing at it with all his strength to get into the house. The puzzled owners let the dog in and he raced for the living room, jumped into the playpen, picked up their year-old son by the seat of the pants, rushed him out of the house and dumped him on the grass. He then barked furiously to get his owners to come out there,

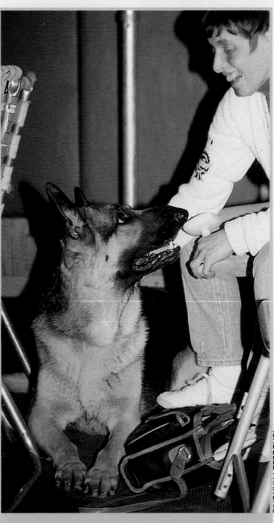

The Shepherd disposition embodies a friendly air, though the breed is discriminate with its trust. As a protector of a shepherd's flock, the breed necessarily could not invest its trust in strangers too readily.

ISABELLE FRANCAIS

too. They did, and in split seconds there was a roaring explosion, and instantly the whole house was aflame. The house and contents were gone before the firemen got there, but the family was safe.

This is no piece of fiction. The story was investigated and run by every news and wire service in the country. But how did the dog know that disaster was imminent? The owners didn't know it. There was no warning of sound or smoke. Why did the dog rescue a baby he hardly even knew? Well, that's German Shepherd character!

SUSPICION OF STRANGERS

Now somewhere along the line you may have been told that a Shepherd is a "one-man dog," a phrase which means just what it says—a dog that will accept no one but his owner, or who is hostile to all others. This term does not apply to the German Shepherd. He is not a one man dog. But while he will be friendly and affectionate with your friends and neighbors whom he knows and sees often, he doesn't like strangers. Any German Shepherd worth feeding is instantly suspicious of strangers! And, in general, he doesn't wish to be patted by strangers. He wants the strangers to commit themselves first. Are they friends of yours, he wants to know? He'll take his cue from you. If you say it's all right—then it's all right with him, and he'll come around and "make up" to the new people. All of which is a perfectly natural extension of a Shepherd's inborn, inbred protectiveness.

ISABELLE FRANCAIS

The breed's natural protective nature applies to children as well as sheep. These Shepherd puppies are getting to know their young keeper, and in no time will be keeping watch over her.

But if you don't like this characteristic in a dog, then don't buy a German Shepherd!

And this same protective instinct carries over to your children. He won't like strangers fooling with them. And if he's in your car, he will sharply resent it if anyone tries to get in it, touch it, or take anything out of it. He is not being silly. He's not being mean. He is showing proper Shepherd character.

But the German Shepherd is essentially a happy dog. He enjoys his training, and he trains so easily. He is happy to do what you want. He's happy to be with you and the family. He's happy to lie quietly or rush around and play. He's happy to go for a walk, and he's happy he has you for an owner. In fact, being as smart as he is, he's probably happy he was born a German Shepherd.

A handsome German Shepherd working on his smile in the great outdoors. The Gumabone® provides hours of entertainment while brightening your dog's teeth and spirits.

EXERCISE AND ENVIRONMENT

The German Shepherd Dog is an all-weather dog, equally at home either in the tropics or in areas of almost constant snow and low temperatures. He adapts himself to any kind of adequate housing in any climate, with no special consideration as far as weather is concerned. In a Shepherd in the tropics may grow one at the usual time, but it will be less heavy. In successive years the undercoat will grow less, and finally stops growing.

OUTDOOR OR INDOOR DOG

The Shepherd, in cold climates, may be kept with perfect safety in

Shepherds do very well in a kennel environment: clean, roomy runs, fresh water, requisite shade and a dog house resort.

ISABELLE FRANCAIS

permanently cold climate or in sections with very cold winters, nature equips him accordingly. On parting the hair of the coat, you will see a dense undercoat of soft, fine hair, which acts as insulation against cold and dampness. Whereas this undercoat usually grows in the early fall in cold climates, the an outside, unheated kennel or building, provided he is fully protected from wind, drafts, and dampness. But if this is to be his life, he must be kept mainly in the cold. He must not be allowed to come into a heated atmosphere for long periods of time and then be put outside. In other words, if he is primarily an outside dog, he

KAREN TAYLOR

Although a Shepherd doesn't need acres and acres to keep him well-exercised and content, no GSD would ever pass up the opportunity to stretch his legs...nor would he pass on a fun game of fetch with his Gumabone® Frisbee®.

must be kept that way.

In extremely hot weather, see to it that he has a cool, shady place to rest during the hottest part of the day. Most importantly, see to it that he has an adequate supply of clean, fresh water readily available at all times. A galvanized pail hung from a hook is ideal if changed often. Be sure, in placing the hook, that the pail is not too high for the dog to reach the last drop of water in the bottom. This is a good setup, however, young dogs seem to love to tip over water pails and make giant mud puddles.

If there is any place to swim in fresh water, encourage your dog to do it. It is both cooling and good exercise. But for this and other exercise, try to limit it to early morning or evening in very hot weather. In general, I believe it is best not to allow a dog to swim in salt water. Although many dogs are not adversely affected, the combination of salt water and sand can result in disorders of the skin and coat.

NEVER CLIP HIS COAT

Good brushing in hot weather is just as important as at any

other time. But don't, under any circumstance, allow yourself to be talked into having your Shepherd clipped or shaved to "make him more comfortable." This is the worst possible thing to do. His coat was put there as protection from direct rays of the sun and for protection against insects, rough ground, and such. Cut off his coat and your dog will probably come down with every skin trouble in the book—and Shepherds almost never have skin troubles. Leave his coat on him!

CITY OR COUNTRY DOG

"Oh I'd love to have a German Shepherd, but I can't. I live in the city in an apartment." This is usually the remark of a person who "just adores" dogs—as long as they belong to somebody else and he isn't concerned with taking proper care of them.

Forget all the nonsense you ever heard about a Shepherd requiring a hundred acres in the country. He doesn't, I tell you, and I have done it for years. You can keep a full-grown Shepherd in a small apartment, and he will enjoy perfect physical and mental health. He is just as happy in the city as he is in the country, providing you are there.

It isn't easy to keep a dog in the city—granted, but it can be done with great success. With a young puppy, it requires eight to ten

After a romp around the estate, this country bumpkin is showing off his new Chooz™ treat.

KAREN TAYLOR

trips to the sidewalk each day. And see to it that you start at once to train your dog to use the gutter, *not* the sidewalk. He'll learn this in two or three days easily. Just guide him into the gutter and hold him there with the leash until he is finished. Then praise him for being a good dog. Be sure to clean up after your dog, as this is required in most places. In addition, he should enjoy walking, say two or three trips around the block.

As your Shepherd matures, the "constitutionals" to the gutter will be cut to two or three a day, in addition to at least an hour, morning and night, of good, brisk leash-walking. If the neighborhood permits, chasing and retrieving a stick or ball is wonderful exercise, as is running and playing with another dog. And while a lot of people may disagree sharply with me on this point, I have found that proper feeding, grooming, and the above exercise is perfectly adequate for a Shepherd to thrive on. Of course, the more exercise the merrier. If you really want a German Shepherd, even though you live in an apartment, you can certainly have one. Just do what has to be done for the dog without thinking of it as a chore. The exercising will be good for you, too. You'll come to enjoy it!

Of course in the suburbs or the country, life is simpler. Your dog can simply go outside into a fenced-in yard.

For dogs who compete in obedience trials, a life in the country is a real plus. There's lots more room to practice for the big event.

ROBERT SMITH

ISABELLE FRANCAIS

ABOVE: A breed as active as the German Shepherd will gain from quality exercise time. A keen and focused temperament is nurtured by plenty of exercise and activity: an active body, an active mind. **BELOW:** Leash training is perhaps the most important aspect of training for city dogs. This Shepherd seems to have his own ideas about walking on lead.

CORINA KAMER

TRAINING

Because of the breed's inherited capacity for training, the German Shepherd puppy in your home is the legitimate heir to a glorious history of service and pleasure to mankind. You owe proper training persons, or whatever possible use he may be put to, the basic training is always the same. Police dog, army dog, guide dog for the blind, all must start with basic obedience—or what might be

Many consider the German Shepherd the most trainable of all dogs. The breed possesses a capacity to learn that is deeply embedded in its heritage.

to your Shepherd. The right and privilege of being trained are his birthright, and no breed of dog trains more readily or more surely than the Shepherd.

Now whether your Shepherd is going to be a handsome, well-mannered housedog and companion, a dog used for herding stock or tracking lost

called "manners training."

Your dog must come instantly when called, and obey the "sit" or "down" command just as fast; he must walk quietly at "heel," whether on or off the lead. He must be mannerly and polite wherever he goes; he must be polite to strangers on the street and in stores. He must be orderly

CORINA KAMER

ABOVE: Hollywood dog trainer Michael Kamer works with a German Shepherd student. Working off-lead is the ultimate test. The dog is told to sit each time the trainer stops. **BELOW:** Kamer demonstrates the heel off-lead. The dog walks close to the trainer's left leg.

CORINA KAMER

in the presence of other dogs. He must not bark at children on roller skates, motorcycles, or other domestic animals. And he

when to come to see the dog. No, he won't forget you, but too frequent visits at the wrong time may slow down his training

Pushing on the dog's rear quarters encourages him to sit. This is but one method of teaching a dog to sit.

CORINA KAMER

must be restrained from chasing cats. It is not a dog's inalienable right to chase cats, and he must be reprimanded for it.

A PROFESSIONAL TRAINER

How do you go about this training? Well, it's a very simple procedure, pretty well standardized by now. First, if you can afford the extra expense, you may send your dog to a professional trainer, where in 30 to 60 days he will learn how to be "a good dog." If you enlist the services of a good professional trainer, follow his advice about

progress. And in using a "pro" trainer you will have to go for some training, too, after the trainer feels your dog is ready to go home. You will have to learn how your dog works and just what to expect of him and how to use what the dog has learned after he is home.

OBEDIENCE TRAINING CLASS

Another way to train your dog (I think this is the best of the three) is to join an obedience training class right in your own community. There is such a group in nearly every community

CORINA KAMER

ABOVE: In addition to learning hand and voice signals for commands, the dog must learn signals for corrections. This dog is being corrected to stay. BELOW: Tapping the dog's toe with your foot is another method of correction. This dog is staying in the down position.

CORINA KAMER

CORINA KAMER

ABOVE: Michael Kamer is instructing the dog to "Go to your place" as he leads him there on leash. BELOW: This is the correction for head up.

CORINA KAMER

nowadays. Here you will be working with a group of people who are also just starting out. You will actually be training your own dog, since all work is under the direction of a head trainer

session! Go early and leave late! Both you and your dog will benefit tremendously.

TRAIN HIM BY THE BOOK

The third way of training your

This Shepherd has been taught "Go to your place" and is now laying contentedly as he awaits the next command.

CORINA KAMER

who will make suggestions to you and also tell you when and how to correct your dog's errors. Then, working with such a group, your dog will learn to get along with other dogs. And, what is more important, he will learn to do exactly what he is told to do, no matter how much confusion there is around him, or how great the temptation to go his own way.

Write to the American Kennel Club for the location of a training club or class in your locality. Sign up. Go to it regularly—every

Successful Dog Training by Michael Kamer has been ranked the best of all training books.

dog is by the book. Yes, you can do it this way and do a good job of it too. But in using the book method, select a book, buy it, study it carefully; then study it some more, until the procedures are almost second nature to you. *Then* start your training. But stay with the book and its advice and exercises. Don't start in and then make up a few rules of your own. If you don't follow the book, you'll get into jams you can't get out of by yourself. If, after a few hours of short training session your dog is still not working as he should, get back to the book for a study session, because it's *your* fault, not the dog's! The procedures of dog training have been so well systematized that it must be your fault, since literally thousands of fine German Shepherds have been trained by the book.

Schutzhund training is not the same as attack training. Schutzhund involves a high degree of skill used over a variety of activities. Sleeve work is but one of the many levels of Schutzhund work.

ROBERT PEARCY

After your Shepherd is "letter perfect" under all conditions, then if you wish, go on to advanced training and trick work. Teach him to track. You never know when a dog with a trained nose can be of great service to your community or to you personally.

FORGET ATTACK TRAINING

Now a word of warning. I have had many inquiries from well-intentioned amateur trainers who want to teach their Shepherds attack and protection work. True, the Shepherd has the brain to do what it is told and to stop when so told, but attack and protection training is *strictly* for experienced trainers of many years' practice. Such a dog, properly trained, is *not* a vicious or unpredictable dog, but he should *never* be owned or kept by a private individual—not ever. Such a dog with the average owner is a highly dangerous weapon. He belongs in military, police, or security forces only—never in private hands. You don't need attack or protection training in your dog, and, in my opinion, you have no right to have a dog so trained.

Your Shepherd will love his obedience training, and you'll burst with pride at the finished product! Your dog will enjoy life even more, and you'll enjoy your dog more. And remember—you owe good training to your German Shepherd!

GROOMING

Your German Shepherd probably requires less grooming than many other breeds of dog. Here again, you can do what is necessary in two minutes, or if you choose, you can make a lengthy theatrical production out of it. Actually, the job is simple and the necessary tools and supplies are few, inexpensive and easy to use.

BATHING RARELY NECESSARY

Let's begin with the subject of washing your Shepherd. This is the simplest problem of all to solve. Just don't wash him. Your dog's coat is so constructed that it is virtually impossible to get dirty. Certainly he can get mud on himself, or paint, or grease. In any case, the soiling is right on the surface of the coat. For mud, the easiest thing to do is squirt a hose on him, or else let the mud dry and get it off with good, hard brushing. For tar, paint, oil, and such, use an appropriate solvent—a little on a cloth—and dab the soiled area with it. If it's a large area, follow the same procedure and then wash him in mild soap and warm water, since

Groom from head to toe. Check your Shepherd's ears for mites or any other parasites.

ISABELLE FRANCAIS

tne cleaning fluid you have used will surely irritate his skin. Rinse him well after using any type of fluid, so that he does not lick off a lethal substance. Surface dirt, in general, may be removed by rubbing the dog with an old rough towel wrung out in hot water. Follow this with a dry rub and brushing. If it should be necessary to wash your dog, take proper care in drying him off, especially in the winter.

In the event your dog runs afoul of a skunk (and I do mean afoul) get him to where you can pour lots of water on him. Since "skunk juice" is oily, water tends to float a good deal of it off. Following the repeated water treatment, soap and rinse him several times. All the smell will have to wear off eventually!

KEEP HIM WELL BRUSHED

For grooming equipment, your Shepherd mostly needs a large, stiff brush. A horse brush is ideal. Apply it vigorously, brushing first from tail to head, then head to tail. Then take a fairly coarse metal comb and comb out the brush of his tail. And that's it.

I have heard people complain that sometimes dogs smell too "doggy." Just what that means, I wouldn't know. But if you think

TRIM NAILS REGULARLY

Now about toenails. Most dogs need their nails cut every two or three months. Your veterinarian might do this for you, but he is a busy medical man, and besides, you should learn to do it yourself.

ISABELLE FRANCAIS

The German Shepherd requires so little in the way of grooming and special care that owners will find they can spend more time doing quality things.

your dog smells "doggy," invest in some of the good "dry bath" liquids or sprays that are on the market. They do help to groom the coat and usually have a pleasant, woodsy smell. Of course, follow the directions for use carefully. If you are fussy, you might follow this procedure once a week. But again, don't wash him. Washing should, in my opinion, be avoided. Undoubtedly it upsets the ideal condition of normal, healthy skin and coat.

It's very easy.

Equip yourself with a dog's nail cutter that looks a little like a ticket punch. There is a hole in the metal where the actual punch would be. This you hold over the tip of the nail and with a quick, hard squeeze on the handles, a flat blade shoots across the tip of the nail, cutting it off. Avoid the pincher or scissors-type nail cutters. They pinch and hurt, and you'll have quite a struggle to complete the job.

Study your dog's nails carefully.

Never allow them to get long, because, aside from any other reason, long nails will ruin his feet. In cutting the nails, work in a strong light with the dog lying flat on his side. Cut off just the tip of the nail for the first few times, until you are skillful at it. Do all four feet, of course, and use care not to cut into the quick. If you do, it may bleed a little, but it usually doesn't require any treatment. If it bleeds a lot, hold

One of the powders that can be dusted into the coat will usually suffice. Follow the package directions carefully.

Dogs rarely pick up lice. However, in the event your dog does, consult your veterinarian. Or, if you live in an area where there is a tick season, it is a matter of going over your dog at least every two days, literally with a fine-tooth comb, to locate and remove small ticks or larger ones that have not

ISABELLE FRANCAIS

Puppies can pick up fleas and ticks from the grass. Be sure to check them carefully after they've been outdoors.

some styptic powder against the nail until the bleeding stops. Try to keep the nails cut back so they extend only a little beyond the line of the paw.

WATCH FOR PARASITES

Occasionally it may happen that your Shepherd will pick up fleas (of course, from that mutt next door!), but there is no cause for alarm. They can be eliminated just as fast as they are picked up. Rarely will an infestation be heavy enough to require a washing with flea soap.

yet attached themselves to the dog's skin. Large ticks that have already burrowed into the skin should be anesthetized with rubbing alcohol and then removed with tweezers and the slight wounds dabbed with some mild antiseptic. Ticks are hard to destroy; it's best to burn them.

Groom your dog as often as possible, once a day or twice a week if possible, but always remember that the health of your dog's skin and coat comes from the inside—from correct feeding.

SHOWING

A show dog is a comparatively rare thing. He is one out of several litters of puppies. He happens to be born with a degree of physical perfection that closely approximates the standard by which the breed is judged in the show ring. Such a dog should, on maturity, be able to win or approach his championship in good, fast company at the larger shows. Upon finishing his championship, he is apt to be as highly desirable as a breeding animal. As a proven stud, he will automatically command a high price for service.

Showing dogs is a lot of fun—yes, but it is a highly competitive sport. While all the experts were once beginners, the odds are against a novice. You will be showing against experienced handlers, often people who have devoted a lifetime to breeding, picking the right ones, and then showing those dogs through to their championships. Moreover, the most perfect dog ever born has faults, and in your hands the faults will be far more evident than with the experienced handler who knows how to minimize his dog's faults. These are but a few points on the sad side of the picture.

The experienced handler, as I say, was not born knowing the ropes. He learned—*and so can you!* You can if you will put in the same time, study and keen observation that he did. But it will take time!

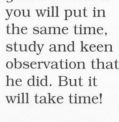

ISABELLE FRANCAIS

Handler Jimmy Moses sets up Ch. Altana's Mystique to show off her best assets. Mystique is the epitome of a show dog: rarely defeated, she won more Bests in Show than any other dog in history.

KEY TO SUCCESS

First, search for a truly fine show prospect. Take the puppy home, raise him by the book, and as carefully as you know how, give him every chance to mature into the dog you hoped for. My advice is to keep your dog out of big shows, even Puppy Classes, until he is mature. Maturity in the male is roughly two years; with the female, 14 months or so. When your dog is approaching maturity, start out at match shows, and with this experience for both of you, then go gunning for the big wins at the big shows.

Next step, read the standard by which the German Shepherd is judged. Study it until you know it by heart. Having done this, and while your puppy is at home (where he should be) growing into a normal, healthy dog, go to every dog show you can possibly reach. Sit at the ringside and watch Shepherd judging. Keep your ears and eyes open. Do your own judging, holding each of those dogs against the standard, which you now know by heart.

In your evaluations, don't start looking for faults. Look for the virtues—the best qualities. How does a given dog shape up against the standard? Having looked for and noted the virtues, then note the faults and see what prevents a given dog from standing correctly or moving well. Weigh these faults against the virtues, since, ideally, every feature of the dog should contribute to the harmonious whole dog.

"RINGSIDE JUDGING"

It's a good practice to make notes on each dog, always holding the dog against the standard. In "ringside judging," forget your personal preference for this or that feature. What does the standard say about it? Watch carefully as the judge places the dogs in a given class. It is difficult from the ringside always to see why number one

American and Canadian Ch. Petracca's Mike winning placement at an outdoor dog show.

NORMAN J. SELDES

was placed over the second dog. Try to follow the judge's reasoning. Later try to talk with the judge after he is finished. Ask him questions as to why he placed certain dogs and not others. Listen while the judge explains his placings, and, I'll say right here, any judge worthy of his license should be able to give reasons.

join the national German Shepherd club and to subscribe to its magazine. From the national club, you will learn the location of an approved regional club near you. Now, when your young Shepherd is eight to ten months old, find out the dates of match shows in your section of the country. These differ from regular shows only in that no

ROBERT SMITH

The German Shepherd proves himself in many rings of competition, for he is highly trainable and enjoys the spotlight.

When you're not at the ringside, talk with the fanciers who have German Shepherds. Don't be afraid to ask opinions or say that you don't know. You have a lot of listening to do, and it will help you a great deal and speed up your personal progress if you are a good listener.

THE NATIONAL CLUB
   You will find it worthwhile to

championship points are given. These shows are especially designed to launch young dogs (and new handlers) on a show career.

ENTER MATCH SHOWS
   With the ring deportment you have watched at big shows firmly in mind and practice, enter your dog in as many match shows as you can. When in the ring, you

have two jobs. One is to see to it that your dog is always being seen to its best advantage. The other job is to keep your eye on the judge to see what he may want you to do next. Watch only the judge and your dog. Be quick and be alert; do exactly as the judge directs. Don't speak to him except to answer his questions. If he does something you don't like, don't say so. And don't irritate the judge (and everybody else) by constantly talking and fussing with your dog.

In moving about the ring, remember to keep clear of dogs beside you or in front of you. It is my advice to you *not* to show your Shepherd in a regular point show until he is at least close to maturity and after both you and your dog have had time to perfect ring manners and poise in the match shows.

Puppies can enter match shows at six months of age, though their training can begin as early as eight weeks of age.

This German Shepherd is undertaking the high jump at an obedience trial.

HEALTH

We know our pets, their moods and habits, and therefore we can recognize when our German Shepherd is experiencing an off-day. Signs of sickness can be very obvious or very subtle. As any mother can attest, diagnosing and treating an ailment require common sense, knowing when to seek home remedies and when to visit your doctor...or veterinarian, as the case may be.

Your veterinarian, we know, is your German Shepherd's best friend, next to you. It will pay to be choosy about your veterinarian. Talk to dog owning friends whom you respect. Visit more than one vet before you make a lifelong choice. Trust your instincts. Find a knowledgeable, compassionate vet who knows German Shepherds and likes them.

Grooming for good health makes good sense. The Shepherd's coat is double and medium in length. The dense outer coat benefits from regular brushing to keep it looking glossy and clean. Brushing stimulates

ROBERT SMITH

Your German Shepherd puppy should be bright eyed and spirited, alert and healthy.

the natural oils in the coat and also removes dead haircoat. Shepherds shed seasonally, which means their undercoat (the soft downy white fur) is pushed out by the incoming new coat. A medium-strength bristle brush and a hound glove are all that is required to groom this natural and beautiful breed of dog.

Anal sacs, sometimes called anal glands, are located in the musculature of the anal ring, one on either side. Each empties into the rectum via a small duct. Occasionally their secretion becomes thickened and accumulates so you can readily feel these structures from the outside. If your German Shepherd is scooting across the floor dragging his rear quarters, or licking his rear, his anal sacs may need to be expressed. Placing pressure in and up toward the anus, while holding the tail, is the general routine. Anal sac secretions are characteristically foul-smelling, and you could get squirted if not careful. Veterinarians can take care of this

The coat on your German Shepherd indicates the health of your dog: it should be glistening and vibrant in color and sheen.

KAREN TAYLOR

during regular visits and demonstrate the cleanest method.

Many German Shepherds are predisposed to certain congenital and inherited abnormalities, such as hip dysplasia, a blatantly common problem in purebred dogs with few exceptions. Unfortunately, the German Shepherd suffers from one of the highest percentage rates of hip dysplasia of any dog. This is due to the breed's unwavering popularity and the careless breeding that surrounds the procreation of such a popular breed. New owners must insist on screening certificates from such hip registries as OFA or PennHIP. Since HD is hereditary, it's necessary to know that the parents and grandparents of your puppy had hips rated good or better. Dysplastic dogs suffer from badly constructed hip joints which become arthritic and very painful, thereby hindering the dog's ability to be a working dog, a good-moving show dog, or even a happy, active pet.

Elbow dysplasia has recently become more of a concern, and the OFA screens for elbows as well. Chronic degenerative radiculomyelopathy, like HD, affects the dog's ability to amble, though is not related. CDRM leads to difficulty for the dog to maneuver his hind legs. This rear-quarter lameness results in worse degeneration, loss of bladder control and finally paralysis. Most animals are put down before the condition becomes this debilitating.

Osteochondritis dissecans affects the bone of many large breeds, and although many other breeds are more prone to this disease, the GSD has been a victim on many occasions. Panosteitis, affecting bone production, as well as hypertrophic osteodystrophy and myasthenia gravis are also reported as potential bone diseases in the Shepherd.

Eye conditions such as pannus, cataracts, retinal dysplasia, and Collie eye have become concerns for Shepherd breeders. Screening for eye problems has therefore been prioritized.

Von Willebrand's disease, a bleeding disorder, and hemophilia A are conditions that affect many dog breeds and do not exclude the German Shepherd.

Certain heart conditions, such as patent or persistent ductus arteriosus and persistent right aortic arch, are concerns in the GSD, though not frequently encountered.

Epilepsy, a possible hereditary condition that is linked to the brain's receiving incorrect stimulus, hinders many breeds of dog and is problematic in Shepherds.

Despite this lengthy list of potential problems, a well-bred Shepherd is a healthy, long-lived companion animal. Proper care and education can only help owners promote the health and longevity of their dogs. Most breeders advise against feeding the German Shepherd one large meal per day because of the dangers of bloat (gastric torsion): the twisting of the stomach causes gas to build up and the organ expands like a balloon. Avoiding strenuous exercise and large amounts of water can preclude the occurrence of bloat, as can feeding two smaller meals instead of one large one. A good commercial dog food is recommended for the dog's balanced diet.

For the continued health of your dog, owners must attend to vaccinations regularly. Your veterinarian can recommend a vaccination schedule appropriate for your dog, taking into consideration the factors of climate and geography. The basic vaccinations to protect your dog are: parvovirus, distemper, hepatitis, leptospirosis, adenovirus, parainfluenza, coronavirus, bordetella, tracheobronchitis (kennel cough), Lyme disease and rabies.

Parvovirus is a highly contagious, dog-specific disease, first recognized in 1978. Targeting the small intestine, parvo affects the stomach, and diarrhea and vomiting (with blood) are clinical signs. Although the dog can pass the infection to other dogs within three days of infection, the initial signs, which include lethargy and depression, don't display themselves until four to seven days. When affecting puppies under four weeks of age, the heart muscle is frequently attacked. When the heart is affected, the puppies exhibit difficulty in breathing and experience crying and foaming at the nose and mouth.

ISABELLE FRANÇAIS

Responsible breeders have each dog screened for possible eye conditions before including that dog in a breeding program.

Distemper, related to human measles, is an airborne virus that spreads in the blood and ultimately in the nervous system and epithelial tissues. Young dogs or dogs with weak immune systems can develop encephalomyelitis (brain disease) from the distemper infection. Such dogs experience seizures, general weakness and rigidity, as well as "hardpad". Since distemper is largely incurable, prevention through vaccination is vitally important. Puppies should be vaccinated at six to eight weeks of age, with boosters at ten to 12 weeks. Older puppies (16 weeks and older) who are unvaccinated should receive no fewer than two vaccinations at three- to four-week intervals.

Hepatitis mainly affects the liver and is caused by canine adenovirus type I. Highly infectious, hepatitis often affects dogs nine to 12 months of age. Initially the virus localizes in the dog's tonsils and then disperses to the liver, kidney and eyes. Generally speaking the dog's immune system is capable of combating this virus. Canine infectious hepatitis affects dogs whose systems cannot fight off the adenovirus. Affected dogs have fever, abdominal pains, bruising on mucous membranes and gums, and experiences coma and convulsions. Prevention of hepatitis exists only through vaccination at eight to ten weeks of age and then boosters three or four weeks later, then annually.

Leptospirosis is a bacterium-related disease, often spread by rodents. The organisms that spread leptospirosis enter through the mucous membranes and spread to the internal organs via the bloodstream. It can be passed through the dog's urine. Leptospirosis does not affect young dogs as consistently as do the other viruses; it is reportedly regional in distribution and somewhat dependent on the immunostatus of the dog. Fever, inappetence, vomiting, dehydration, hemorrhage, kidney and eye disease can result in moderate cases.

Bordetella, called canine cough, causes a persistent hacking cough in dogs and is very contagious. Bordetella involves a virus and a bacteria: parainfluenza is the most common virus implicated; *Bordetella bronchiseptica*, the bacterium. Bronchitis and pneumonia result in less than 20 percent of the cases, and most dogs recover from the condition within a week to four weeks. Non-prescription medicines can help relieve the hacking cough, though nothing can cure the condition before it's run its course. Vaccination cannot guarantee protection from canine cough, but it does ward off the most common virus responsible for the condition.

Lyme disease (also called borreliosis), although known for decades, was only first diagnosed in dogs in 1984. Lyme disease can affect cats, cattle, and horses, but especially people. In the U.S., the disease is transmitted by two ticks carrying the *Borrelia burgdorferi* organism: the deer tick (*Ixodes scapularis*) and the western black-legged tick (*Ixodes pacificus*), the latter primarily affects reptiles. In Europe, *Ixodes ricinus* is responsible for spreading Lyme. The disease causes lameness, fever, joint swelling, inappetence, and lethargy. Removal of ticks from the dog's coat can help reduce the chances of Lyme, though not as much as avoiding heavily wooded areas where the dog is most likely to contract ticks. A vaccination is available, though it has not been proven to protect dogs from all strains of the organism that causes the disease.

Rabies is passed to dogs and people through wildlife: in North America, principally through the skunk, fox and raccoon; the bat is not the culprit it was once thought to be. Likewise, the common image of the rabid dog foaming at the mouth with every hair on end is unlikely the truest scenario. A rapid dog exhibits difficulty eating, salivates much and has spells of paralysis and awkwardness. Before a dog reaches this final state, it may experience anxiety, personality changes, irritability and more aggressiveness than is usual. Vaccinations are strongly recommended as rabid dogs are too dangerous to manage and are commonly euthanized. Puppies are generally vaccinated at 12 weeks of age, and then annually. Although rabies is on the decline in the world community, tens of thousands of humans die each year from rabies-related incidents.

Parasites have clung to our pets for centuries. Despite our modern efforts, fleas still pester our pet's existence, and our own. All dogs itch, and fleas can make even the happiest dog a miserable, scabby mess. The loss of hair and habitual biting and chewing at themselves rank among the annoyances; the nuisances include the passing of tapeworms and the whole family's itching through the summer months. A full range of flea-control and elimination products are available at pet shops, and your veterinarian surely has recommendations. Sprays, powders, collars and dips fight fleas from the outside; drops and pills fight the good fight from inside. Discuss the possibilities with your vet. Not all products can be used in conjunction with one another, and some dogs may be more sensitive to certain applications than others. The dog's living quarters must be debugged as well as the dog itself. Heavy infestation may require multiple treatments.

Always check your dog for ticks carefully. Although fleas can be acquired almost anywhere, ticks are more likely to be picked up in heavily treed areas, pastures or other outside grounds (such as dog shows or obedience or field trials). Athletic, active, and hunting dogs are the most likely subjects, though any passing dog can be the host. Remember Lyme disease is passed by tick infestation.

As for internal parasites, worms are potentially dangerous for dogs

Pet stores sell a wide variety of top-quality shampoos specially designed for use on dogs. A medicated shampoo is particularly helpful if the dog is suffering from minor itching or the like. Photograph courtesy of Hagen.

and people. Roundworms, hookworms, whipworms, tapeworms, and heartworms comprise the blightsome party of troublemakers. Deworming puppies begins at around two to three weeks and continues until three months of age. Proper hygienic care of the environment is also important to prevent contamination with roundworm and hookworm eggs. Heartworm preventatives are recommended by most veterinarians, although there are some drawbacks to the regular introduction of poisons into our dogs' system. These daily or monthly preparations also help regulate most other worms as well. Discuss worming procedures with your veterinarian.

Roundworms pose a great threat to dogs and people. They are found in the intestine of dogs and can be passed to people through ingestion of feces-contaminated dirt. Roundworm infection can be prevented by not walking dogs in heavy-traffic people areas, by burning feces, and by curbing dogs in a responsible manner. (Of course, in most areas of the country, curbing dogs is the law.) Roundworms are typically passed from the bitch to the litter, and bitches should be treated along with the puppies, even if she tested negative prior to whelping. Generally puppies are treated every two weeks until two months of age.

Hookworms, like roundworms, are also a danger to dogs and people. The hookworm parasite (known as *Ancylostoma caninum*) causes cutaneous larva migrans in people. The eggs of hookworms are passed in feces and become infective in shady, sandy areas. The larvae penetrate the skin of the dog, and the dog subsequently becomes infected. When swallowed, these parasites affect the intestines, lungs, windpipe, and the whole digestive system. Infected dogs suffer from anemia and lose large amounts of blood in the places where the worms latch onto the dog's intestines, etc.

Although infrequently passed to humans, whipworms are cited as one of the most common parasites in America. These elongated worms affect the intestines of the dog, where they latch on, and cause colic upset or diarrhea. Unless identified in stools passed, whipworms are difficult to diagnose. Adult worms can be eliminated more consistently than the larvae, since whipworms exhibit unusual life cycles. Proper hygienic care of outdoor grounds is critical to the avoidance of these harmful parasites.

Tapeworms are carried by fleas, and enter the dog when the dog swallows the flea. Humans can acquire tapeworms in the same way, though we are less likely to swallow fleas than dogs are. Recent studies have shown that certain rodents and other wild animals have been infected with tapeworms, and dogs can be affected by catching and/or eating these other animals. Of course, outdoor hunting dogs and terriers are more likely to be infected in this way than are your typical house dog or non-motivated hound. Treatment for tapeworm has proven very effective, and infected dogs do not show great discomfort or symptoms. When people are infected, however, the liver can be seriously damaged. Proper cleanliness is the best bet against tapeworms.

Heartworm disease is transmitted by mosquitoes and badly affects the lungs, heart and blood vessels of dogs. The larvae of *Dirofilaria immitis* enters the dog's bloodstream when bitten by an infected mosquito. The larvae takes about six months to mature. Infected dogs suffer from weight loss, appetite loss, chronic coughing and general fatigue. Not all affected dogs show signs of illness right away, and carrier dogs may be affected for years before clinical signs appear. Treatment of heartworm disease has been effective but can be dangerous also. Prevention as always is the desirable alternative. Ivermectin is the active ingredient in most heartworm preventatives and has proven to be successful. Check with your veterinarian for the preparation best for your dog. Dogs generally begin taking the preventatives at eight months of age and continue to do so throughout the non-winter months.

Puppies acquire their immunity from their mother. Once a puppy has been weaned from its mother it must be vaccinated against infectious diseases.

KAREN TAYLOR

FEEDING

Now let's talk about feeding your German Shepherd, a subject so simple that it's amazing there is so much nonsense and misunderstanding about it. Is it expensive to feed a German Shepherd? No, it is not! You can feed your German Shepherd economically and keep him in perfect shape the year round, or you can feed him expensively. He'll thrive either way, and let's see why this is true.

First of all, remember a German Shepherd is a dog. Dogs do not have a high degree of selectivity in their food, and unless you spoil them with great variety (and possibly turn them into poor, "picky" eaters) they will eat almost anything that they become accustomed to. Many dogs flatly refuse to eat nice, fresh beef. They pick around it and eat everything else. But meat—bah! Why? They aren't accustomed to it! They'd eat rabbit fast enough, but

they refuse beef because they aren't used to it.

The Nylabone®/Gumabone® Pooch Pacifiers enable the dog to slowly chew off the knobs while they clean their own teeth. The knobs develop elastic frays which act as a toothbrush. These pacifiers are extremely effective as detailed scientific studies have shown.

VARIETY NOT NECESSARY

A good general rule of thumb is forget all human preferences and don't give a thought to variety. Choose the right diet for your German Shepherd and feed it to him day after day, year after year, winter and summer. But what is the right diet?

Hundreds of thousands of dollars have been spent in canine nutrition research. The results are pretty conclusive, so you needn't go into a lot of experimenting with trials of this and that every other week. Research has proven just what your dog needs to eat and to keep healthy.

DOG FOOD

There are almost as many right diets as there are dog experts, but the basic diet most often recommended is one that consists of a dry food, either meal or kibble form. There are several of excellent quality, manufactured by reliable companies, research tested, and nationally advertised. They are inexpensive, highly satisfactory, and easily available in stores everywhere in containers of five to 50 pounds. Larger amounts cost less per pound, usually.

If you have a choice of brands, it is usually safer to choose the better known one; but even so, carefully read the analysis on the package. Do not choose any food in which the protein level is less than 25 percent, and be sure that this protein comes from both animal and vegetable sources. The good dog foods have meat meal, fish meal, liver, and such, plus protein from alfalfa and soybeans, as well as some dried-milk product. Note the vitamin content carefully. See that they are all there in good proportions; and be especially certain that the food contains properly high levels of vitamins A and D, two of the most perishable and important ones. Note the B-complex level, but don't worry about carbohydrate and mineral levels. These substances are plentiful and cheap and not likely to be lacking in a good brand.

The advice given for how to choose a dry food also applies to moist or canned types of dog foods, if you decide to feed one of these.

Having chosen a really good food, feed it to your German Shepherd as the manufacturer directs. And once you've started, stick to it. Never change if you can possibly help it. A switch from one meal or kibble-type food can usually be made without too much upset; however, a change will almost invariably give you (and your German Shepherd) some trouble.

WHEN SUPPLEMENTS ARE NEEDED

Now what about supplements of various kinds, mineral and vitamin, or the various oils? They are all okay to add to your German Shepherd's food. However, if you are feeding your German Shepherd a correct diet, and this is easy to do, no supplements are necessary unless your German Shepherd has been improperly fed, has been sick, or is having puppies. Vitamins and minerals are naturally present in all the foods; and to ensure against any loss through processing, they are added in concentrated form to the dog food you use. Except on the advice of your veterinarian, added amounts of vitamins can prove harmful to your German Shepherd! The same risk goes with minerals.

FEEDING SCHEDULE

When and how much food to give your German Shepherd? As to when (except in the instance of puppies), suit yourself. You may feed two meals per day or the same amount in one single feeding, either morning or night. As to how to prepare the food and how much to give, it is generally best to follow the directions on the food package. Your own German Shepherd may want a little more or a little less.

Fresh, cool water should always be available to your German Shepherd. This is important to good health throughout his lifetime.

ALL GERMAN SHEPHERDS NEED TO CHEW

Puppies and young German Shepherds need something with resistance to chew on while their teeth and jaws are developing—for cutting the puppy teeth, to induce growth of the permanent teeth under the puppy teeth, to assist in getting rid of the puppy teeth at the proper time, to help the permanent teeth through the gums, to ensure normal jaw development, and to settle the permanent teeth solidly in the jaws.

The adult German Shepherd's desire to chew stems from the instinct for tooth cleaning, gum massage, and jaw exercise—plus the need for an outlet for periodic doggie tensions.

This is why dogs, especially puppies and young dogs, will often destroy property worth hundreds of dollars when their chewing instinct is not diverted from their owner's possessions. And this is why you should provide your German Shepherd with something to chew—something that has the necessary functional qualities, is desirable from the German Shepherd's viewpoint, and is safe for him.

It is very important that your German Shepherd not be permitted to chew on anything he can break or on any indigestible thing from which he can bite sizable chunks. Sharp pieces, such as from a bone which can be broken by a dog, may pierce the intestinal wall and kill. Indigestible things that can be bitten off in chunks, such as from shoes or rubber or plastic toys, may cause an intestinal stoppage (if not regurgitated) and bring painful death, unless surgery is promptly performed.

Strong natural bones, such as 4- to 8-inch lengths of round shin bone from mature beef—either the kind you can get from a butcher or one of the variety available commercially in pet stores—may serve your German Shepherd's teething needs if his mouth is large enough to handle them effectively. You may be tempted to give your German Shepherd puppy a smaller bone and he may not be able to break it when you do, but puppies grow rapidly and the power of their jaws constantly increases until maturity. This means that a growing German Shepherd may break one of the smaller bones at any time, swallow the pieces, and die painfully before you realize what is wrong.

All hard natural bones are very abrasive. If your German Shepherd is an avid chewer, natural bones may wear away his teeth prematurely; hence, they then should be taken away from your dog when the teething purposes have been served. The badly worn, and usually painful, teeth of many mature dogs can be traced to excessive chewing on natural bones.

Contrary to popular belief, knuckle bones that can be chewed up and swallowed by your German Shepherd provide little, if any, usable calcium or other nutriment. They do, however, disturb the digestion of most dogs and cause them to vomit the nourishing food they need.

Dried rawhide products of

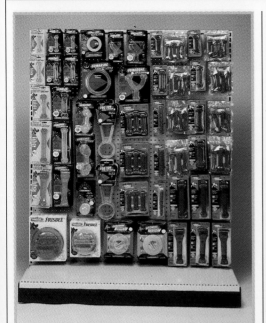

Most pet shops have complete walls dedicated to safe pacifiers.

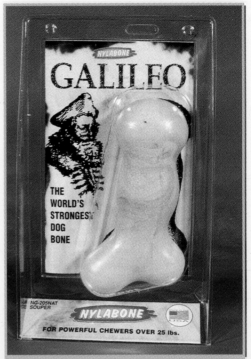

The Galileo is an extremely tough nylon pacifier. Its design is based upon original sketches by Galileo. A book explaining the history and workings of the design comes inside each package. This might very well be the best design for German Shepherds.

German Shepherds have such strong jaws that most ordinary pacifiers (chew devices) are immediately destroyed. The Hercules has been designed with German Shepherds and other large breeds in mind. This bone is made of polyurethane, like car bumpers.

Raised dental tips on each dog bone works wonders with controlling plaque in German Shepherds.

Only get the largest Plaque Attacker™ for your German Shepherd.

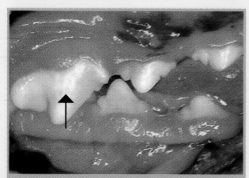

In a scientific study, this shows a dog's tooth while being maintained by Gumabone® chewing.

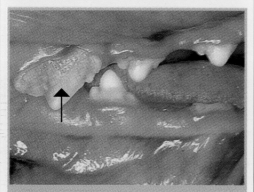

The Gumabone® was taken away and in 30 days the tooth was almost completely covered with plaque and tartar.

various types, shapes, sizes, and prices are available on the market and have become quite popular. However, they don't serve the primary chewing functions very well; they are a bit messy when wet from mouthing, and most German Shepherds chew them up rather rapidly—but they have been considered safe for dogs until recently. Now, more and more incidents of death, and near death, by strangulation have been reported to be the results of partially swallowed chunks of rawhide swelling in the throat. More recently, some veterinarians

have been attributing cases of acute constipation to large pieces of incompletely digested rawhide in the intestine.

A new product, molded rawhide, is very safe. During the process, the rawhide is melted and then injection molded into the familiar dog shape. It is very hard and is eagerly accepted by German Shepherds. The melting process also sterilizes the rawhide. Don't confuse this with pressed rawhide, which is nothing more than small strips of rawhide squeezed together.

The nylon bones, especially

The nylon tug toy is actually a dental floss. You grab one end and let your German Shepherd tug on the other as it slowly slips through his teeth since nylon is self-lubricating (slippery). Do NOT use cotton rope tug toys as cotton is organic and rots. It is also weak and easily loses strands which are indigestible should the dog swallow them.

those with natural meat and bone fractions added, are probably the most complete, safe, and economical answer to the chewing need. Dogs cannot break them or bite off sizable chunks; hence, they are completely safe—and being longer lasting than other things offered for the purpose, they are economical.

Hard chewing raises little bristle-like projections on the surface of the nylon bones— to provide effective interim tooth cleaning and vigorous gum massage, much in the same way your toothbrush does it for you. The little projections are raked off and swallowed in the form of thin shavings, but the chemistry of the nylon is such that they break down in the stomach fluids and pass through without effect.

The toughness of the nylon provides the strong chewing resistance needed for important jaw exercise and effectively aids teething functions, but there is no tooth wear because nylon is non-abrasive. Being inert, nylon does not support the growth of microorganisms; and it can be washed in soap and water or it can be sterilized by boiling or in an autoclave.

Nylabone® is highly recommend-ed by veterinarians as a safe, healthy nylon bone that can't splinter or chip. Nylabone® is frizzled by the dog's chewing action, creating a toothbrush-like surface that cleanses the teeth and massages the gums. Nylabone®, the only chew products made of flavor-impreg-nated solid nylon, are available in your local pet shop. Nylabone® is super-ior to the cheaper bones because it is made of virgin nylon, which is the strongest and longest-lasting type of nylon available. The cheaper bones are made from recycled or re-ground nylon scraps, and have a tendency to break apart and split easily.

Chocolate Nylabone®: before and after. Once your dog's bone looks like this one (bottom), it's time to replace it.

Nothing, however, substitutes for periodic professional attention for your German Shepherd's teeth and gums, not any more than your toothbrush can do that for you. Have your German Shepherd's teeth cleaned at least once a year by your veterinarian (twice a year is better) and he will be happier, healthier, and more pleasant to live with.

YOUR NEW PUPPY

SELECTION

When you do pick out a German Shepherd puppy as a pet, don't be hasty; the longer you study puppies, the better you will understand them. Make it your transcendent concern to select only one that radiates good health and spirit and is lively on his feet, whose eyes are bright, whose coat shines, and who comes forward eagerly to make and to cultivate your acquaintance. Don't fall for any shy little darling that wants to retreat to his bed or his box, or plays coy behind other puppies or people, or hides his head under your arm or jacket appealing to your protective instinct. *Pick the German Shepherd puppy who forthrightly picks you! The feeling of attraction should be mutual!*

DOCUMENTS

Now, a little paper work is in order. When you purchase a purebred German Shepherd puppy, you should receive a transfer of ownership, registration material, and other "papers" (a list of the immunization shots, if any, the puppy may have been given; a note on whether or not the puppy has been wormed; a diet and feeding schedule to which the puppy is accustomed) and you are welcomed as a fellow owner to a long, pleasant association with a most lovable pet, and more (news)paper work.

GENERAL PREPARATION

You have chosen to own a particular German Shepherd puppy. You have chosen it very carefully over all other breeds and all other puppies. So before you ever get that German Shepherd puppy home, you will have prepared for its arrival by reading everything you can get your hands on having to do with the management of German Shepherds and puppies. True, you will run into many conflicting opinions, but at least you will not be starting "blind." Read, study, digest. Talk over your plans with your veterinarian, other "German Shepherd people," and the seller of your German Shepherd puppy.

When you get your German Shepherd puppy, you will find that your reading and study are far from finished. You've just scratched the surface in your plan to provide the greatest possible comfort and health for your German Shepherd; and, by the same token, you do want to assure yourself of the greatest possible enjoyment of this wonderful creature. You must be ready for this puppy mentally as well as in the physical requirements.

TRANSPORTATION

If you take the puppy home by car, protect him from drafts, particularly in cold weather. Wrapped in a towel and carried in the arms or lap of a passenger, the German Shepherd puppy will usually make the trip without mishap. If the pup starts to drool and to squirm, stop the car for a few minutes. Have newspapers handy in case of car-sickness. A covered carton lined with newspapers provides protection for puppy and car, if you are driving alone. Avoid excitement and unnecessary handling of the puppy on arrival. A German Shepherd puppy is a very small "package" to be making a complete change of surroundings and company, and he needs frequent rest and refreshment to renew his vitality.

THE FIRST DAY AND NIGHT

When your German Shepherd puppy arrives in your home, put him down on the floor and don't pick him up again, except when it is absolutely necessary. He is a dog, a real dog, and must not be lugged around like a rag doll. Handle him as little as possible, and permit no one to pick him up and baby him. To repeat, *put your German Shepherd puppy on the floor or the ground and let him stay there except when it may be necessary to do otherwise.*

Quite possibly your German Shepherd puppy will be afraid for a while in his new surroundings, without his mother and littermates. Comfort him and reassure him, but don't console him. Don't give him the "oh-you-poor-itsy-bitsy-puppy" treatment. Be clam, friendly, and reassuring. Encourage him to walk around and sniff over his new home. If it's dark, put on the lights. Let him roam for a few minutes while you and everyone else concerned sit quietly or go about your routine business. Let the puppy come back to you.

Playmates may cause an immediate problem if the new German Shepherd puppy is to be greeted by children or other pets. If not, you can skip this subject. The

Retractable leashes are a nice option for walking your dog. Of course, first the dog requires training on a standard leash before you should afford him this much leeway. Photograph courtesy of Hagen.

natural affinity between puppies and children calls for some supervision until a live-and-let-live relationship is established. This applies particularly to a Christmas puppy, when there is more excitement than usual and more chance for a puppy to swallow something upsetting. It is a better plan to welcome the puppy several days before or after the holiday week. Like a baby, your German Shepherd puppy needs much rest and should not be over-handled. Once a child realizes that a puppy has "feelings" similar to his own, and can readily be hurt or injured, the opportunities for play and responsibilities provide exercise and training for both.

Taking the puppy outdoors to his special place after every meal is one method of housebreaking the puppy.

For his first night with you, he should be put where he is to sleep every night—say in the kitchen, since its floor can usually be easily cleaned. Let him explore the kitchen to his heart's content; close doors to confine him there. Prepare his food and feed him lightly the first night. Give him a pan with some water in it—not a lot, since most puppies will try to drink the whole pan dry. Give him an old coat or shirt to lie on. Since a coat or shirt will be strong in human scent, he will pick it out to lie on, thus furthering his feeling of security in the room where he has just been fed.

HOUSEBREAKING HELPS

Now, sooner or later—mostly sooner—your new German Shepherd puppy is going to "puddle" on the floor. First take a newspaper and lay it on the puddle until the urine is soaked up onto the paper. *Save this paper.* Now take a cloth with soap and water, wipe up the floor and dry it well. Then take the wet paper and place it on a fairly large square of newspapers in a convenient corner. When cleaning up, always keep a piece of wet paper on top of the others. Every time he wants to "squat," he will seek out this spot and use the papers. (This routine is rarely necessary for more than three days.) Now leave your German Shepherd puppy for the night. Quite probably he will cry and howl a bit; some are more stubborn than others on this matter. But let him stay alone for the night. This may seem harsh treatment, but it is the best procedure in the long run. Just let him cry; he will weary of it sooner or later.

VERSATILITY

When one thinks of a Seeing Eye dog for a blind person, an image of the German Shepherd comes into the mind. When picturing a search and rescue team at a post-tornado site, one sees German Shepherds leading the hunt. Ask someone what type of dog is a police dog, and he will reply, "German Shepherd," without hesitation. There is no other breed in the world that is as versatile as the German Shepherd Dog. The GSD serves society in more ways and in greater numbers than every other breed put together. In fact, 90 percent of all service dogs in the world are German Shepherds. The ability to guard, hunt, pull, run, and reason has made the GSD useful in a wide range of jobs and activities. The extraordinary talents of the GSD, along with its easy trainability, almost overshadow the breed's genuine beauty—all together, the German Shepherd is quite an impressive dog.

With such a dazzling dog, it should be a crime not to make use of its talents. Remember, however, that although the GSD is a brilliant dog capable of almost any canine job, a dog can only be as smart as its trainer. A dog of this stature deserves to be treated with the utmost respect, and part of that respect is knowing when you are in over your head. There are some skills, such as obedience, that can and should be taught by the average dog owner.

However, there are a number of other jobs, such as guard dog training, that require training by a professional. To give you an idea of what this breed is capable of, the following is an overview of the multi-purpose skills of the German Shepherd Dog.

MILITARY DOGS

Since the earliest dates of history, the dog has been employed by armies to aid in their fighting. In modern times, canine soldiers have been used by French and German armies in World War I and by the US Army in WWII. These army dogs were utilized in a number of different roles: they served as sentries and guards of prisoners, defended camps from enemies, detected mines, worked with rescue units, found wounded soldiers, and carried food and medicine. One interesting function the dog served in wartime was delivering messages across enemy lines, with the idea that even if the dog was caught, he could not be made to talk, whereas a human messenger could.

The US Army made use of German Shepherds in at least two serviceable roles where they performed impressively. As scout dogs, the German Shepherds were able to detect enemy presence from 250 yards away—thus preventing possible ambushes. In further making use of their fine scenting ability, the GSDs were also used to sniff out land mines.

The German Shepherd is so effective in this capacity that demonstrations have shown that one dog can find more explosives in 20 minutes than a hundred men could find in three hours.

POLICE DOGS

Some of these same skills have been adjusted to apply to peacetime, as the GSD has found worldwide work as a police dog. This concept has been especially appealing to under-funded, under-manned police forces who can use all the help they can get at low cost. By training a dog, you can't get much better help without paying a salary! Not only is a police dog cost-efficient, but also highly effective—most criminals would almost rather be shot than have to tangle with the ferocious jaws of an angry German Shepherd. The police officers themselves also like the idea of having canine companions because in the case of pursuit, the dog will get the man and either hold him or bring him back alive; a bullet can never be called back. And because they have such cool nerves and are very controllable, German Shepherds are used with great efficiency in controlling riots and other violent disturbances. Besides patrolling the streets and crime-fighting, the GSD also provides extensive abilities in other areas of law enforcement. For example, the German Shepherd Dog's excellent scenting ability allows him to aid bomb squads in sniffing out explosives, in search and rescue work for finding injured people, in arson squads in finding accelerants, in airports and customs for detecting drugs and other illegal contraband, and in countless other areas performing similar duties.

SCHUTZHUND

Schutzhund is a German word that means "protection dog." It is a training and competition program that develops and tests a dog's abilities as a protection dog. Schutzhund trials have been held throughout the world since the early 1900s and include temperament, obedience, alertness, tracking, and protection tests. Each entry in a Schutzhund trial is scored according to their performance and must exhibit the following attributes: complete obedience despite distraction; courage, confidence, and dependability in protection; and scenting ability, determination, and concentration while tracking. A dog must earn at least 70 points out of a possible 100 in both obedience and tracking and at least 80 points out of 100 in protection, passing all three phases in the same trial to earn a title. The titles, or degrees, are SchH I (beginner level), SchH II (intermediate level), and SchH III (master level). Once a dog has achieved a level, the title is added to the end of the dog's name. Other degrees that can be accomplished and added to the dog's name are *Wachshunde* (WH) or watchdog; *Fahtenhundprufung* (FH) or advanced tracking; *Ausdauerprufung* (AD), which is a 20-kilometer endurance test; and

Verkehrssichere Begleithunde(VB), which is a traffic-sure companion dog test. In Germany, these trials and their dogs are taken so seriously that a GSD cannot be bred until it has proved itself in Schutzhund. Dogs involved in Schutzhund/protection training should not be confused with attack-trained dogs. Schutzhund training is based on obedience and the dog's ability to follow his master's commands, while attack dogs are generally less versed in formal obedience.

WATCHDOG

Looking at the GSD's history as a military and police dog, it makes sense that the German Shepherd is an effective watchdog for the home and family. Although the GSD is not a particularly aggressive dog, it can become very attached to, and protective of, its family and property. This protective nature is the main characteristic that makes the GSD such a good watchdog. Combine this protectiveness with a keen alertness that has been tested and trusted by military groups all over the world, plus the intimidating size and ferocious bark, and

ISABELLE FRANCAIS

The classic police dog, the German Shepherd is a watchdog par excellence as well as a devoted family companion.

you can see why the GSD is an ideal watchdog.

GUIDE DOGS

On the lighter side of things, the German Shepherd Dog has brains to go with his brawn. The high intelligence of the breed was the main reason the GSD was the first dog used as a guide dog for the blind and later the deaf. Originally used as guide dogs for blind World War I veterans, the GSD's abilities led to the establishment of the Seeing Eye Foundation in 1929. This initial organization and others like it made the GSD the breed of choice for guiding the blind and deaf. Being someone else's eyes or ears requires incredible concentration, composure in the face of distractions, responsibility, the intelligence to make decisions, and the good sense to avoid dangerous situations. The German Shepherd possesses all of the aforementioned abilities, and that is why it has been used from the beginning as the preeminent choice as a guide dog.

SERVICE DOGS

Similarly, the GSD can be very serviceable to people living with detrimental diseases and injuries such as cerebral palsy, multiple sclerosis, muscular dystrophy, and paralysis. Such persons have a difficult time executing the simplest tasks, such as picking up dropped keys, opening a door, answering the telephone, pushing an elevator button, or getting up from a chair. Since it is nearly impossible to have human aid 24 hours a day, the next best thing is a well-trained support dog. In most cases, the dog needed must be strong and sturdy enough to pull people in wheelchairs up steep inclines, carry groceries, and deter muggers. The support dog must also be bright enough to answer a telephone when it rings and hand it to its master, pick up a coin that has dropped to the ground, and fetch specified objects such as a pencil, book, or glove. The multi-talented German Shepherd can accomplish all of these tasks and hundreds more for a handicapped person, and thus the person can achieve an otherwise unknown independence and confidence.

Intelligence, beauty and affection too. These qualities recommend the German Shepherd as a pet, a guardian, a performance animal as well as a service dog.

R. HUTCHINS

Along the same lines, the calm and patient nature of the GSD has made it ideal as a therapy dog, benefiting the sick and the elderly. Most hospitals and nursing homes allow and encourage visits by dogs to lift up the spirits of their patients. German Shepherds and other dogs that participate in therapy programs are family pets that have been properly socialized and conditioned to be touched by strangers and are able to handle accidental abuse by frightened or awkward patients. The GSD's steady nerves and high pain threshold come in handy when applied in this role.

The publisher wishes to acknowledge the following owners and handlers for their cooperation with the photographers who provided images for this book:

Susan A. Ewart, Jane A. Firestone, Margaret Lash, Roberta Laufer, James A. Moses, Joseph Petracca, Roberta Rebhon, Virginia Stewart, Vicki Taylor, Bob Touchette, Jamie Walker, Robin K. Wescher and Ruth Zieleniewski.